# Bucky the Farting Easter Bunny's Butt Blasts

Humor Heals Us

# Bucky the Farting Easter Bunny's Butt Blasts

By Humor Heals Us

One day while delivering eggs,
I got caught in a trap.
On Easter Day, of course!
It was a **big** mishap.

Let me tell you the story.
I was hopping along,
Humming and tooting to the tune
Of my **favorite** song.

Then I saw some candy
Dangling there for me to eat.

So I grabbed it.
It tasted so **sweet**.

Before I knew it,
The door shut with a **BANG**!

When I shook the cage,
All I could hear was Clang, clang!

The hours passed.
I almost gave up
Until I saw my friend
Piper The Pup.

"Here are some fries.
Try pooting your way out!"
So I did what he said
But it wouldn't POP out.

Froggy was passing along.
What happened to you, Buddy?
I'm stuck and I can't escape.
Help me! I'll pay you **money**.

"Here's some cupcakes,
Try tooting your way out!"
So I did what she said,
But it wouldn't come out!

Chickity Chic hopped by.
"What's all the **fuss**?"
Help me out of this cage
Before I turn to dust.

"I think I've got something
That will help you.
I know you don't like veggies,
But the **carrots** might do."

Thank you, Chickity Chic!
Yummy yum yum!
Carrots are so good
To my **tummy tum tum**!

I chewed them up quickly.
After I was done eating
Chickity Chic said to me,
"Now try farting!"

So I pointed my butt
To the cage door.
I held on tight to the bars
And gave it a **push** once more

And WHOOSH! Just like that,
The door blew apart.
My friends were blasted
In a **stormy** whirlwind fart.

They were happy
That I was finally free.
And we all picnicked
Under the big tree.

Follow us on FB and IG @humorhealsus
To vote on new title names and freebies, visit
us at humorhealsus.com for more information.

@humorhealsus          @humorhealsus

www.ingramcontent.com/pod-product-compliance
Lightning Source LLC
Chambersburg PA
CBHW042024090426
42811CB00016B/1727

9 781637 311325